SEASHORE

BOWLS

FAILURE

GUMMY BEARS

UNDER THE SEA

FOOTBALL

SUNFLOWERS

SCHOOL

SHORT BOOKS

NIGHTFALL

When the night falls

The stars will call

They appear in the sky

When the sun says goodbye

The moon rises

These are the prizes

Night falls day or night

Hope the ghouls do not give me a fright

SEASHORE

The shells sit there

While crabs are bare

The water washes up on the shore

While kids become poor

Ice cream sells quick

Children take their pick

The seashore is a wonderful place

That does not take up much space

<u>**BOWLS**</u>

MUCH SO PASTA GOOD

M   E

Y   V

B   O

O   L

W   I

L **ITS FULL OF PASTA**

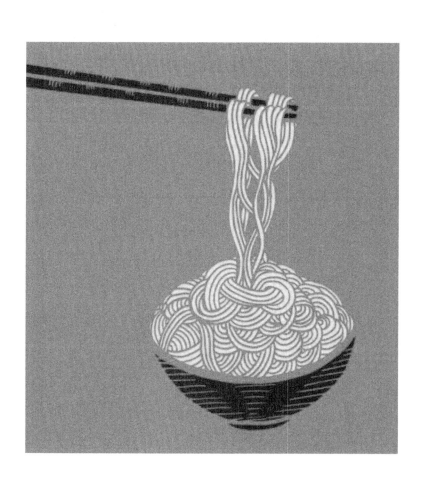

FAILURE

People fail when they really try

Sometimes they will cry

Failure can lead to hate

Hopefully they will not discombobulate

The failure may change

Even though it may cause pain

GUMMY BEAR

Chewy sticky and a good taste

Unless they have no paste

The song gets stuck in your head

Makes me want to go to bed

UNDER THE SEA

Under the sea are a lot of things

Like sea monkeys and crabs that fling

Side to side they jump

As the sea snails sit in a clump

Mermaids swim around gracefully

While the ships sail peacefully

FOOTBALL

All the teams we support

Liverpool, Arsenal and Westhamster court

Kicking the ball around

As it rolls on the ground

As it scores in the goal

The pub screams as the keeper kicks the pole

SUNFLOWERS

Yellow blossom like the sun

They sway in the wind as the breeze pushes past

The bees are having some guaranteed fun

Tiny cute children running around fast

Now the winter has begun

The summer quickly surpassed

Its shot by like a bullet from a gun

It was the one sunflower that lasts

SCHOOL

Math, English and French

The kids sit down on the bench

They run and run around

While they fall over on the playground

SHORT BOOKS

Short books annoy me

But one she likes to write

These short books

But they all feel like crooks

Just like me

BETH STEVENS

I am a young writer who one day wants to be an author, this is my first ever poem book.

It was quite hard to write, I am drafting a novel and decided to write these while I was doing that.

Printed in Great Britain
by Amazon